· WC
ENCOU

Footstools for faith

by
Selwyn Hughes

Further study section compiled by
Trevor J. Partridge

© Selwyn Hughes 1987

Material originally published in Every Day With Jesus in 1982 and 1984

ISBN 1 85345 003 0

**CWR, 10 Brooklands Close, Windmill Road,
Sunbury-on-Thames, Middx TW16 7DX**
Illustrations by Norman Savine
Cover photo: Ace Photo Agency/Ian Reynolds
Typeset by Creative Editors & Writers Ltd, Watford
Printed by Crusade Printing, Chertsey

DAY 1

Grace — 'tis a charming sound
PSALM 84:1–12

"Blessed are those whose strength is in you…" (v. 5: NIV)

The great Baptist preacher C.H. Spurgeon spoke of "footstools for our faith to kneel upon". If we allow God's grace to strengthen us, life's trials can become such footstools for faith to kneel where there was little or no faith before. By looking for God's will at times of trial and seeing His work in our lives reflecting His perfect love, we can grow in strength and faith. We can kneel on these footstools before His throne. During the next four weeks we will be looking at some of the difficulties that, by God's grace, can be transformed into footstools.

God's grace does not weaken our personalities but strengthens them. In John 4:14 Jesus said, "But the water that I shall give him shall be in him a well of water springing up into everlasting life." Now note: "the water that I shall give … shall be … a well … springing up." The gift produces spontaneity and self-expression. Many gifts do not — they weaken rather than strengthen. Indeed, it is hard to give to some people because you know that by so doing you weaken rather than reinforce them. But the grace of God is a gift that strengthens and develops a person, and brings them to a place of independent dependency.

When we receive the gift of God's grace, it is not a gift that demands nothing on our part. It is, perhaps, the most expensive gift we can ever receive — expensive to us. For when we take it — *fully* take it — we have to give our all in exchange. Once we give ourselves to God, then comes mutuality. We are no longer nonentities — we are co-operating persons. "At the very moment we bend lowest," said a famous theologian, "we stand straightest." Those who depend most on the grace of God develop the strongest personalities. So when we receive God's grace, and allow it to pulse through our personalities, we become, not clinging, dependent types, but men and women who, as John Powell puts it, are "fully human and fully alive".

PRAYER: Blessed Lord Jesus, may Your grace ever enable me to turn life's trials into footstools for faith to kneel upon before You. Thank You, dear Jesus. Amen.

FURTHER STUDY: Acts Ch. 16; Matt. 19:26; Lk. 1:37
1 *How did Paul respond to God's grace?* 2 *What was the result?*

DAY 2

The footstool of temptation
1 CORINTHIANS 10:1–13

> "...for he has promised this and will do what he says. He will show you how to escape temptation's power..." (v. 13: TLB)

We turn now to consider one such footstool for faith to kneel upon — *temptation*. Perhaps at this very moment you are surrounded by a host of powerful temptations which threaten to engulf your soul. But, take heart, our text for today tells us that God is committed to giving you the strength to face the most fierce of temptations. You will find a footstool for faith.

Note what the text says: "He has promised this and will do what he says." God owes it to Himself, His Word, His character and His love to succour you in any temptation that threatens to overwhelm your soul. He knows that you can do nothing without Him, and that you will certainly fail if He abandons you. The truth is that if God was to remove Himself from you in the critical moments when you are overtaken by a strong and fierce temptation, then He would not be true to Himself. So drop your anchor right now into the depths of this reassuring and encouraging revelation: "He has promised this and will do what he says." Or, in other words, you *will* find a footstool for faith.

The faithfulness of God's promise does not consist in delivering us from temptation but in never allowing the temptation to go beyond our power to resist. God knows infinitely better than we do just how much strength we have, and in the most amazing way He moderates the activities of the Tempter, and will never permit him to attack us with more strength than we have to resist. This is not all — He will increase the power of His assistance in proportion to the strength of the temptation. And that's a promise!

PRAYER: O Father, I am so thankful that I am not alone in this battle against temptation. I see that success in meeting temptation comes, not by mastering certain techniques, but in being mastered by certain convictions — the conviction that You will support me in every temptation. Thank You, Father. Amen.

FURTHER STUDY: Matt. 4:1–11; Heb. 2:18; 2 Pet. 2:9
1 *How did Jesus handle temptation?* 2 *What was the Father's response?*

DAY 3

Unbeatable and unbreakable
ISAIAH 54:11–17

"**…no weapon turned against you shall succeed…**" (v. 17: TLB)

We continue examining the subject of turning temptation into a footstool for our faith. We saw yesterday that God is committed to strengthening us to face every temptation that comes our way, and He has promised that He will not permit one temptation to come to us that we cannot handle. Temptation, though we may not think so when we face it, has a useful purpose. As we grapple, we grow. Goethe said, "Difficulties prove men." They do. We must learn to do more with temptation than just bear it — we must learn to use it. The secret of using temptation, and turning it to our advantage, is one of life's greatest secrets. Once we have learned it we are unbeatable and unbreakable.

A Christian schoolteacher once told me that when she was talking to her class about the Cross, one little girl raised her hand and said, "Jesus didn't just carry His Cross — He *used* it." "*Out of the mouths of babes and sucklings*"! What a powerful truth lies in the words of that little girl. God doesn't want us to just bear the cross of temptation: He wants us to use it. You can't bear a cross for long unless you use it. A stoic bears a cross; a Christian uses it and makes it bear him.

We must, therefore, make a decision before we go any further: are we simply going to bear temptation or are we going to use it? When we view temptation with the right attitude, and face it with the strength and grace that God provides, then the things that oppose us contribute to our advancement. I once heard the singer, Sammy Davis Jnr, take words that were shouted to him from the audience and set them to music. Someone read out a shopping list which he promptly set to a tune! It's not what comes, it's what you do with it that matters.

PRAYER: O Father, I see so clearly that when I am in You, and You are in me, then everything can be used — even temptation. Your grace enables me to be unbeatable and unbreakable. I am so thankful. Amen.

FURTHER STUDY: 1 Jn Ch. 5; Rev. 12:9–11; 2 Cor. 2:11, 11:3; 1 Thess. 3:5
1 *What is the victory that overcomes the world? 2 What are two aspects of this?*

DAY 4

"It hurts good"
JAMES 1:1–8

"…is your life full of … temptations? Then be happy, for when the way is rough, your patience has a chance to grow." (vv. 2–3: TLB)

We are saying that when we find ourselves confronted by temptation, God finds a way of supplying us with sufficient grace that makes the temptation a footstool for our faith to kneel upon. Everything, temptation included, can be taken and used for higher ends when God is in it. That is why a true Christian ought not to be nonplussed, for everything can be made to work toward favourable ends. A young Army officer, involved in the Falkland Islands dispute, was asked by a television reporter, "But isn't the weather unfavourable?" He replied, "Weather in war is always favourable — providing you know how to use it." That is the point — everything can contribute if you know how to use it.

Philosophers have told us repeatedly that life is determined more by our reactions than by our actions. Temptation sweeps in upon us and forces its way into our lives without our asking (and sometimes without our acting), and it is then that reaction plays an important part. We can react in self-pity and frustration or we can act with confidence and with courage, and make the temptation work to improve our character and deepen our hold upon God. Thus it becomes a footstool for our faith. Temptation may contain an evil design but by the time you have finished with it, the evil has been turned into good.

The South American Indians like bitter medicine. They don't consider it beneficial unless it has an acrid taste. "It hurts good," they say. You can make temptation 'hurt good' when you see in it the possibilities of increasing your dependency upon God and developing your character, moulding it into the image of Jesus Christ.

PRAYER: Lord Jesus, You who faced the bitterness of temptation and of the Cross, and used that bitterness to make You better, strengthen me by Your grace so that I, too, can follow Your example and turn every temptation into a triumph. For Your own dear Name's sake. Amen.

FURTHER STUDY: Jas. 4:1–8; Eph. 6:11; 1 Pet. 5:8
1 *What is the 5 point plan to overcome temptation?* 2 *What does God supply?*

DAY 5

Why God allows it
JAMES 1:9–20

"Blessed is the man who perseveres under trial, because when he has stood the test, he will receive the victor's crown…" (v. 12: NIV)

Today we examine the question: Why does God allow temptation? In order to answer that we must look at the Greek word for temptation used in the New Testament — *peirasmos*. It means to test, to try or to prove. The Biblical use of the word (unlike the modern use of it) does not contain the idea of seduction or entrapment, but rather the putting of a person to a test for the purpose of deepening their personal qualities. The purpose, then, behind every temptation is the development of our character.

One writer says, "The conversion of a soul is the work of a moment, but the making of a saint is the work of a lifetime." Oswald Chambers, expressing the same truth but in a different way, said, "God can, in one single moment, make a heart pure, but not even God can give a person character." Character would not be the precious thing it is if it could be acquired without effort, without combat and without contradictions. "Virtue that has not been tried and tested," said one great theologian, "is not worthy of the name of virtue." It is essential, in a world such as this, that temptation comes to try the people of God, for without temptation there can be no advancement, no development, no growth in character.

The question may arise in your mind: "What is character?" "Character," as someone aptly put it, "is what we are in the dark." Reputation is what other people think of us — character is what we are on the inside. Character is the strength and refinement of soul that we develop as we stand against the tide of temptation. As I said the day before yesterday: as we grapple, we grow. And out of the growing comes character.

PRAYER: O Father, if character is something achieved rather than acquired, then help me in the achieving. And if temptation is the way by which You deepen my character, then I welcome it — in Your Name. Amen.

FURTHER STUDY: Job Chs. 1–2, 13:15, 17:9, Ch. 42
1 *What was Job's attitude?* 2 *How did it develop character?*

DAY 6

Why fear it?
1 PETER 1:1–9

"These have come so that your faith ... may be proved genuine..." (v. 7: NIV)

To many people the idea of God allowing His children to be tempted by the devil is inconsistent with His omnipotence. "If God is almighty," they reason, "then He should intervene in Satan's attempts to seduce us and prevent him from having access to our personalities." However, it is because God is omnipotent that He permits us to be tempted.

F.P. Harton says, "A conquering nation that is not sure of its own strength refuses to allow the people it subjects any kind of independence at all, and keeps control with a strong hand — but the real reason is fear." God does not control His universe through fear but through eternal love and justice. Although God allows men and women to be tempted for the express purpose of building character, He ensures that to each one there flows a stream of grace that, when received, enables the person to overcome the temptation and use it to higher ends.

One of the devil's strategies in attacking God's children is to attempt to persuade them that God is not able to help them in time of temptation. God is well able to help them, and He helps, not so much by extricating them from the temptation, but by supplying them with sufficient grace to use it and overcome it. Temptation is part of God's purposes for us here on earth, so why fear it? If humility does not allow us to desire temptation, because that would be to presume on our own strength, then zeal for our Christian development does not allow us to dread it, still less to be unhappy when it comes. Holiness and purity of soul would not be as awesome to our carnal nature if they could be acquired without effort.

PRAYER: Lord, I see that You seek to deliver me from all that would stain my soul and sour my spirit. And temptation is one way that this can be achieved. So help me to face it in Your strength, and recognise that it has a beneficial purpose. Amen.

FURTHER STUDY: Zech. Ch. 13; Job 23:10; Psa. 66:10; Isa. 48:10; 1 Pet. 4:12–13
1 *How should we respond in the day of refining?* 2 *What is the result?*

DAY 7

Making our problems His own
HEBREWS 2:5–18

"Because he himself suffered when he was tempted, he is able to help those who are being tempted." (v. 18: NIV)

We continue thinking through this matter of why God allows us to be tempted.

When God designed us in the beginning He made us with the awesome power of choice — with the possibility that we might go astray and break our own hearts as well as His. What if God had made us without the power of choice, or with the power to choose only the good? Well, this would not really have been choice, because choice obviously involves choosing between one thing and another. If we could choose only the good, then there would be no such thing as character, for character involves freedom of choice — the freedom to choose either the good or the evil. Kant said, "There is nothing in the world, or even out of it, that can be called good, except a good will." You see, if there is no will, there is no personality, and where there is no personality, there is no sense of goodness and badness.

In a way, God, in desiring to give man freedom of choice, embarked upon a risky project. Yet, as one theologian points out, "Parents take the same risk when they bring a child into the world. The child may go astray and crush their lives — and his own." But parents assume that risk. And why? Because they determine that they will do their best for their child, and make that child's problems their very own. Parents accept the fact that having children involves suffering and pain, especially when the children decide to go contrary to their expectations and wishes. However, parenthood accepts this cross — it cannot do otherwise. So it is with God. In creating us, He knew He would have to make our problems His own; and this He did, all glory to His wonderful Name, when He wore our flesh, endured our temptations and gave Himself for us on that blood-soaked tree.

PRAYER: O Father, how can I ever sufficiently thank You for making my problems Your very own. You are truly a wonderful Parent — and I am grateful more than words can convey. Amen.

FURTHER STUDY: 1 Pet. Ch. 2; Isa. 53:12; Heb. 9:28, 4:15–16
1 *What did Jesus do when reviled?* 2 *Why can we approach His throne boldly?*

DAY 8

The highest petition
MATTHEW 6:5–15

"…lead us not into temptation…" (v. 13)

We must face one more question before we finish discussing temptation: should we take any steps to prepare ourselves to meet temptation or should we just go into it head-on, trusting God to help us overcome it? Well, the text before us today suggests that we ought to pray to be kept from all temptation. However, is that what it is really saying? I get more letters about this one text than any other in the Bible. The phrase is the last petition in the Lord's Prayer. I used to think it an anti-climax but now I see it as the highest petition of all.

We know, from what we have seen, that temptation can be a means in God's hands of increasing our faith — it can become a footstool for our faith. Why then should we ask not to be led into it? I am convinced that what Jesus meant by these words is that we should think in terms of being kept from *unrecognised* temptation. When temptation is recognised it can be resisted, for as we absorb the corresponding stream of grace that God has promised accompanies all temptation, we can overcome it and even use it.

However, temptation is not always easily discerned. Simon Peter is an example of this. In the Garden of Gethsemane he was over-confident, but Jesus warned him, "Watch and pray so that you will not fall into temptation" (Matt. 26:41, NIV). But Peter didn't heed that word, and later, when temptation came in the form of a little maid, he cursed and swore and denied his Lord. Peter had not done what the Lord had advised him — "Watch and pray so that you will not fall into temptation." We must recognise our human tendency to stumble on in blind folly, and so we need always to pray: "Lead us not into (unrecognised) temptation."

PRAYER: Lord Jesus, help me to avoid Simon Peter's mistake, and to be ever prayerful and watchful so that I recognise temptation whenever it comes, and whatever form it takes. For Your own Name's sake I pray. Amen.

FURTHER STUDY: Psa. 91:1–16; Lk. 10:19; 2 Cor. 2:10–11; Heb. 2:18
1 *What are some "fowler's snares"?* 2 *How can we guard against Satan's devices?*

DAY 9
The footstool of silence
GALATIANS 1:13–24

"...I did not consult any man ... I went immediately into Arabia..." (vv. 16–17: NIV)

We move now to consider turning *spiritual silence* into a footstool for faith to kneel upon. What do I mean? Well, from time to time many of us enter a situation where it seems that the heavens are silent, and God no longer speaks to us. We are not conscious of any sin, but it seems that God is far away, and nothing we do brings Him closer to us. We enter a period of silence and inactivity; and this is sometimes harder to bear than positive suffering. Are you in such a position right now? I have been there many times, and take it from me — there is grace available to meet this situation.

Someone has said that pauses in music are "music in the making". There is a momentary pause, or silence, that produces a

suspense, making the music more lovely than before. Is it possible that these pauses in our spiritual experience, these enforced silences, may become music in the making? I believe it is.

We often talk of the public life and ministry of Jesus, but little is said concerning what theologians call "the silent years". The call to give His message to the world must have burned like fire in the heart of our Lord during those years of His teens and into His twenties. Just picture it — making yokes for the farmers of Galilee when He yearned to strike the yoke of sin from the neck of humanity! Making ploughs to till the soil when He longed to plough deep furrows in men's and women's hearts! But He did not chafe. He could wait — yes, for thirty long years. Thirty years of silence: three years of song. But what a song; it was richer for the silence that preceded it.

PRAYER: O Father, help me yet again to absorb the grace that flows into my times of silence, so that when I am released, my life will be all the richer. For Jesus' sake. Amen.

FURTHER STUDY: Lam. Ch. 3; Psa. 77:9, 88:8–9
1 *List some of the feelings of the writer.* 2 *List his affirmations concerning the Lord.*

DAY 10

It happened to me
HEBREWS 13:5–21

"…For God has said, 'I will never, *never* fail you nor forsake you.'" (v. 5: TLB)

We continue looking at why God sometimes produces pauses or silences in our lives. These can represent "music in the making" and prepare us for further and finer music.

A couple of years ago I went through such a spiritual pause myself. it seemed for a while as if the heavens were brass, and I wondered whether or not God had lost His voice. Why wouldn't He speak to me? Why wasn't I hearing from heaven as I usually did? Then I remembered that, despite my feelings of isolation and abandonment, the promise that He would never leave me nor forsake me was unimpeachable. He was in my soul, whether my feelings registered it or not. Grace flowed into my heart, and I soaked it up.

During this period the time came around for me to sit down and write *Every Day with Jesus* (it takes me about two or three weeks to write each time), but day after day, as I put my paper into the typewriter and waited — nothing came. Some days I would sit before the typewriter for hours without typing a single word. It got to such a stage that I wondered whether God was drying up the ministry through *Every Day with Jesus*, and that He might want me to turn to other things. The silence in my soul would have been intolerable had I not realised that the pause was for a purpose. I waited, and then one day I heard His voice again. He said to me, as He said to John in Revelation, "What thou seest … write." I began to write, and what I wrote in that particular edition of *Every Day with Jesus* affected more people than many of the others put together. Now, whenever I sense a divine pause, I tremble with excitement for I know that it is but "music in the making".

PRAYER: Father, help me to hold steady when my life goes into a spiritual pause, and help me to be patient under the restriction and turn it into a footstool for my faith before Your throne. For Jesus' sake. Amen.

FURTHER STUDY: Matt. 26:57—28:20; Jn. 2:18–22
1 *How did the disciples respond to God's silence?* 2 *What happened when the silence was broken?*

DAY 11

For the Body of Christ
1 CORINTHIANS 14:26–33

"Let the prophets speak ... and let the other judge." (v. 29)

Today I want to share with you what I believe is a word of prophecy which God gave me as I began this page. As all prophecy has to be judged on its quality and tone, I offer it to you, the Body of Christ, in that spirit. This is the word the Lord gave me concerning spiritual silence:

"I know how your heart fears and trembles at silences, but do not be afraid, my child, for I am at its centre, as well as at its circumference. You feel as if you have been pushed aside, and that I no longer have any purpose for you. But that is not the case. You are precious to me, more precious than any of the world's resources; yes, more precious than the gold or silver that is buried in the mountains and in the hills. Do not let the silence of the moment persuade you that I am no longer interested in you, for you are mine and I am yours. Nothing shall ever break the bond that is between us, for I have washed you in my blood, and with my own hand have written your name in the Book of Life. In the hour of silence you shall know a serenity that you can never know in any other situation.

"The age that rushes by you is like a clap of thunder, and in it you will never find peace. I am not in the thunder of the world's busyness, but I am in the silence. And you shall find me there. I have watched your frantic efforts to achieve, your earnest desires to move ahead, but I have halted them for the moment that I might speak to you. Your time is mine and my time is yours. Let us share it together. The things you expected to happen have not happened because I have hindered them — purposely. Together, in the silence, we shall share, and you shall come forth, in the days that lie ahead, with renewed strength and vitality, and then my purpose for you shall be achieved."

PRAYER: Thank You, dear Lord — thank You. Amen.

FURTHER STUDY: 1 Ki. 19:9–21; Job 34:29; Eccl. 3:7
1 *How did God speak to Elijah?* 2 *What was the result?*

| DAY 12 | **When evil thoughts oppress** MATTHEW 15:1–20 |

"For out of the heart come evil thoughts…" (v. 19: NIV)

We turn now to focus on yet another difficulty that can become a footstool for faith — *the affliction of evil thoughts.* I am thinking, not simply of an occasional wrong thought popping into one's mind, but those situations where people become oppressed by thoughts which are obsessive and repetitive. A letter I received some time ago said, "My private discussions with Christians of all denominations have led me to believe that more are afflicted and oppressed by evil thoughts than we might imagine."

When the late Dr Sangster, the great Methodist preacher, once visited Bexhill-on-Sea, he found a lovely avenue of trees. A nature lover to the core, he walked admiringly up and down the avenue, and then noticed a strange thing. Two of the trees were dead, and not only dead, but dismally and evilly offensive. Frost could not account for it; their neighbours were all healthy. He made enquiries, and found out that the gas main which ran underneath them had been leaking! Everything on the surface had been in their favour — the sea breezes, sunshine, rain ... but they had been poisoned from beneath.

There are many Christians like that. Perhaps you are one. The circumstances of their lives all seem in their favour — a good job, a happy family, a pleasant environment, a fine church, yet their lives are mysteriously blighted by evil thoughts. Who can help us when our lives are spoiled by continual and oppressive evil thoughts? Jesus can! Christ can not only heal the affliction but make it a footstool for faith to kneel upon.

PRAYER: O Father, I am so grateful that week by week You are showing me Your indomitable way. You can do more than sustain me in my weakness; You can turn my weakness into strength. Make me strong in this area. For Jesus' sake. Amen.

FURTHER STUDY: Matt. 5:27–28, 6:19–34; 2 Cor. 10:5; Eph. 4:22–24
1 *List eight ways in which Satan seeks to attack our minds.* 2 *What is the Christian antidote?*

DAY 13

"Be careful, little eyes"
MARK 9:42–50

"And if your eye causes you to sin, pluck it out..." (v. 47: NIV)

Today we come to grips with the question: what are the principles we must follow if we are to move from weakness to strength in relation to this matter of evil thoughts? The first principle is this: *Take steps to ensure that you are not contributing to the problem by the literature you read or the things you watch.*

One great philosopher said that if you want to evaluate the moral tone of a nation or a society, just examine the literature

they read. These days it is hardly possible to pick up a newspaper or a magazine that does not contain a picture or an article that is calculated to inflame our passions. We live in an age which is preoccupied with sensuality and hedonism (the pursuit of pleasure). Any discussion on this subject must inevitably be linked with sex, as this is one of the main ingredients in the problem of evil thoughts. Although sex is not evil in itself, few topics can so engross the mind or kindle our curiosity. People with a hot passionate nature, however high their ideals, often fight a battle in their mind and imagination with sexual fantasies. These, in turn, make them the kind of people of whom Montaigne speaks with much contempt: "Men and women whose heads are a merry-go-round of lustful images."

Fix it firmly in your mind that the first step to victory over evil thoughts is to cut off the supply at the source. Burn any books or magazines in your possession that others might describe as 'really hot'. Turn off the TV when it violates Biblical standards. Avoid newspapers that go in for nudity. Saying 'no' to sensuality is the same as saying 'yes' to God.

PRAYER: Father, help me to realise that although Christianity is a privilege and not a prohibition — it does have prohibition in it. Today I am going to make up my mind to say a firm 'no' to the things that are not of You. Strengthen me in this resolve. Amen.

FURTHER STUDY: 2 Sam. 11:1–17; 1 Jn. 2:16; Lk. 11:34; Eph. 1:18
1 *What was the source of David's downfall?* 2 *List six ways in which Satan tempts us through our eyes.*

DAY 14: The pathway to sin is short
ROMANS 8:1–17

"To set the mind on the flesh is death, but to set the mind on the Spirit is life and peace." (v. 6: RSV)

We continue to look at the principles we can use when evil thoughts crowd unbidden into our minds. *Although it may be impossible to prevent evil thoughts from entering your mind, make a conscious decision not to entertain them.* A well-worn phrase, which I am sure you will have heard before, puts the same thought in this way: you can't stop the birds from flying into your hair, but you can prevent them from building nests.

Burns, the famous poet, said that when he wished to compose a love song, his recipe was to put himself on 'a regimen of admiring a beautiful woman'. He deliberately filled his mind with pictures that were extremely dangerous to his passionate nature. Shairp, his biographer, said of him, "When the images came to be oft repeated, it cannot have tended to his peace of heart or his purity of life." Augustine, one of the great early Christians, also trod this dangerous path. He came to Carthage with its tinselled vice and began at once to coax his own carnal appetites. He said: "I loved not as yet, yet I loved to love; and with an hidden want I abhorred myself that I wanted not. I befouled, therefore, the spring of friendship with the filth of concupiscence, and I dimmed its lustre with the hell of lustfulness; and yet, foul and dishonourable as I was, I craved, through an excess of vanity to be thought elegant and vain. I fell; precipitately then."

Augustine's experience, like that of many others, goes to show the folly of entertaining evil thoughts and desires. Make a firm resolution, then, that although you may not be able to stop evil thoughts crowding into your mind, you will not play host to them.

PRAYER: Father, although I know what I should do, it is often hard — though not impossible — to do it. I give my will to You again today. Take it and strengthen it, so that it will do Your bidding. In Jesus' Name I pray. Amen.

FURTHER STUDY: Psa. 119:1–11, 139:23–24; Prov. 23:7; Matt. 22:37; Phil. 4:8
1 *When do evil thoughts become sin?* 2 *How can we use our thought life productively?*

DAY 15

The law of reversed effort
HEBREWS 2:5–18

"But we see Jesus…" (v. 9: NIV)

Yesterday we stressed the folly of playing with evil thoughts and desires, and we said that although it is sometimes impossible to prevent them from entering our minds, we must make sure we do not entertain them. This sounds good in theory, but how does it work in practice? *Build within your mind a strong picture of Jesus, and when an evil thought comes into your mind, turn and look at Him.*

Those who study the functions of the mind tell us that evil thoughts are not driven out by dwelling on them, even guiltily or prayerfully. It is bad tactics to direct sustained attention to them, even in penitence, for then you experience what is called the *law of reversed effort*. This law states that "the more attention you focus on avoiding something, the more likely you are to hit it". A simplified form of this happens when a cyclist sees a pothole ahead of him, and concentrates on avoiding it — only to run into it.

The longer things are held in the focus of attention, the deeper they are burned into the memory and the more mental associations they make. The way to overcome them is to outwit them by swiftly directing the mind to some other absorbing theme. It may be difficult to dismiss them, but they can be elbowed out by a different and more powerful idea. And what better idea than to hold a picture of Jesus in your mind, reinforced by daily Bible meditation and prayer, so that in the moment of overwhelming testing, the mind is turned towards Him. One who developed this technique into a fine art, said: "Christ in the heart and mind is the safeguard. To think of Him is to summon His aid. Evil thoughts dissolve in the steady gaze of His searching eyes."

PRAYER: O God, my Father, help me develop in my mind and imagination such a powerful picture of Jesus that it will become the saving focus of my being. Help me turn to Him immediately whenever evil thoughts crowd my mind. For Jesus' sake. Amen.

FURTHER STUDY: Jas. 4:1–8; 1 Pet. 5:8–9; Eph. 6:11
1 *What are the three steps James gives for overcoming Satan's attacks?*
2 *How does this apply to wrong thoughts?*

DAY 16

The Word to the rescue
PSALM 119:1–16

"I have hidden your word in my heart that I might not sin against you." (v. 11: NIV)

Another important principle to follow in developing a plan to overcome oppressive and evil thoughts is this: *store up the Word of God in your mind so that it becomes readily available in times of need.*

I have often stressed the importance of this and I make no apology for coming back to it again, as it is one of the most powerful and successful principles of Christian living. Sometimes people write to me and say: "Your practical suggestions are very interesting and intriguing, *but do they work?*" I have one answer: try them and see! They most certainly work for me, and I am absolutely sure that if you apply them in the way I am suggesting, they will work for you, too.

A minister who was away from home on a preaching visit was provided by the church with accommodation in one of the city's large hotels. One night, while going up in the lift, a woman accosted him and suggested that they should spend the night together. "This was more than an evil thought," said the minister, "it was an evil thought clad in the most beautiful and attractive woman I have seen for a long time. I was lonely and she was available." He went on, "But do you know what immediately flashed into my mind? Not my wife and four children — at least not at first. Not even my position and reputation. No, and not even the thought that I might be found out. The thing that immediately rose up within me was an instant visual replay of Romans 6:11–12, 'Consider yourself dead to sin, but alive to God in Christ Jesus.'" The memorised verse came to the rescue — right on time.

PRAYER: Gracious Father, help me to have Your Word so deeply hidden in my heart that it triggers an automatic reaction within me whenever I am threatened by evil. For Jesus' sake. Amen.

FURTHER STUDY: Psa. 119:17–40; Jer. 23:29; Eph. 6:17; Heb. 4:12
1 *How can we hide God's Word in our hearts?* 2 *How can we use the weapon God has given us?*

DAY 17
The last thought at night
PSALM 4:1–8

"I will lie down and sleep in peace, for you alone, O Lord, make me dwell in safety." (v. 8: NIV)

Today we look at the principle of *letting your last thought at night be a thought about your Lord and Saviour Jesus Christ.*

The last thoughts that lie on our minds at night are powerful and determinative, for the door into the subconscious is opening and they drop in to work good or evil. It's bad enough struggling with evil thoughts while you are awake: don't let them take control while you are asleep. Your conscious mind may be inactive while you are asleep; not so the subconscious. The last thoughts lying in your mind as you go to sleep usually become the 'playthings' of the subconscious, and it works on these during the hours you are asleep.

If it is true that your mind is active while you are asleep, and there certainly seems to be plenty of evidence to support this theory, then make your mind work in a positive and not a negative way. Satan delights to drop an evil thought into your mind during the moments immediately prior to sleep, because he knows that it will work destructively all through the night, influencing your attitudes and most likely preventing you from enjoying a peaceful night's sleep. Then when you wake, you find that not only do you have to face the problems of another day, but you have to face them without having drawn fully on the resources available to you through sleep. Thus begins a recurring pattern which cannot help but drag you down. So learn to elbow out any evil thought that

enters your mind when about to go to sleep, and let your last thought be a thought of Christ.

PRAYER: Father, if it is true that my mind works when I am asleep, then help me to make it work for good and not for evil. Teach me the art of holding a thought about You on my mind immediately prior to going to sleep. I shall begin tonight, Lord. Amen.

FURTHER STUDY: Gen. Ch. 1 & 24:63; Psa 1:1–6, 63:6
1 *When does God's day start?* 2 *Why is it important to meditate on God's Word at night?*

DAY 18

Moving together into victory
2 PETER 1:3–11

"...make every effort to add to your faith ... self-control..." (vv. 5–6: NIV)

We examine one more principle in relation to this matter of overcoming oppressive and persistent evil thoughts: *God is willing to do His part in helping you in this battle with evil thoughts — but you must be willing to do yours.*

There is a teaching in some Christian circles that if we discover a need for change in our lives, we should passively wait upon God until He accomplishes it. It sounds so spiritual, but actually it borders on profound error. A Christian man once said to me: "I would like to be free from a certain sin I am involved in, but I find I am powerless to break away from it." I asked him what he expected to happen in order for him to find deliverance. He said, "I expect God to take away the desire for this sin and thus set me free." Can you see what he was doing? He was saying, in effect, "God is responsible for delivering me, and my task is to wait *passively* until He does so."

Let me tell you, that view is unbiblical — and what is more, it doesn't work. Although deliverance comes from God, *we are the ones that carry it out.* Let that sink in! The principle is this — you supply the willingness, and He will supply the power. Do you really want to win this battle against evil thoughts? If so, you can. Show God you mean business by putting the principles you have learned this week into practice, and you will pave the way for His miraculous power to work in and through you. Once you have done this, life's oppressive and evil thoughts will never be able to break you again. Here, too, you can become strong at the broken place.

PRAYER: Gracious Father, thank You for reminding me that deliverance is a team-effort. It involves the Holy Spirit and me. I supply the willingness: You supply the power. So let's team up, Father, and move together into victory. Amen.

FURTHER STUDY: Dan. Ch. 1; Rom. 6:13; Eph. 6:13
1 *How did Daniel and his friends deal with temptation?* 2 *What were the results of their resisting temptation?*

DAY 19
Coming back from doubt
JOHN 20:19–31

"Thomas said to him, 'My Lord and my God!'" (v. 28: NIV)

This week we consider another problem that through God's grace can become a footstool for faith — *the area of deep and disturbing doubts*. All men and women who are entrusted with caring for people know of those who have received Christ as their Saviour and Lord, but yet are afflicted with paralysing doubts. Some of these people go through deep agony of soul as they wrestle inwardly with doubt, ending up spiritually exhausted.

I met someone like this recently. She told me that she was a scientist and had serious doubts about certain parts of the Scriptures. "I'm afraid that one day I will wake up," she said, "and discover that science has disproved large chunks of Scripture." I could sympathise with her problem, but really her doubts were quite unfounded. Science, that is, *real* science, will never disprove Scripture, only confirm it. Half-baked science may appear to discredit the truth of God's Word, but real science can only validate it.

I suppose the classic example of doubt is found in the disciple Thomas. We call him 'doubting Thomas' — an unfair label if ever there was one. It's sad how we pick out a negative in a person and label him for that one thing. Thomas had his moment of doubt, but he came back from that place of weakness with strong faith. How strong? Let history judge. A well-authenticated tradition has it that Thomas went to India and founded a strong church there. Even today there are Christians in India who call themselves by his name — the St Thomas Christians. They are some of the finest Christians I have ever met. Thomas had his doubts allayed in one glorious moment of illumination — and then he went places. So can you!

PRAYER: O my Father, just as You took Thomas and changed him from a doubter to a man of amazing faith and achievement — do the same for me. For Your own dear Name's sake I ask it. Amen.

FURTHER STUDY: Psa. 37:1–40; Isa. 12:2; Lk. 12:29
1 List seven steps of trusting given in verses 1–9 of this psalm. 2 What are five results of trusting?

DAY 20

Truth — in the inner parts
PSALM 51:1–19

"Surely you desire truth in the inner parts..." (v. 6: NIV)

Today we face the question: what do we do when we find ourselves assailed by honest doubts? Well, firstly, *we must learn to distinguish between honest doubts and defensive doubts.*

Many of the doubts that trouble Christians concerning aspects of the Christian faith are made half-consciously into a screen to hide some moral weakness or failure. I am not denying that some people experience acute intellectual problems in relation to their faith, and it would be arrogant to suggest, or even hint, that everyone troubled by doubts is consciously or unconsciously using them as a screen. But because experience has shown that some do, this issue has to be faced. So, difficult though it may be, ask yourself now: am I using my doubts as a 'defence mechanism' to cover up some weakness or personal defect? A 'defence mechanism', by the way, is a device employed by our minds to prevent us from facing up to reality.

Adam used a defence mechanism when he blamed Eve for his sin. It is called *projection* — refusing to face up to personal responsibility, and projecting the blame on to someone else. Could it be that some of your doubts may be due to this? I am not suggesting, of course, that they *are*, but they *could be*. If you are willing to look at this issue objectively, or perhaps with the help of a wise and responsible Christian friend, then, I assure you, God will not withstand your plea. One hymnwriter said:

> "Jesus the hindrance show,
> Which I have feared to see
> Yet let me now consent to know
> What keeps me out of Thee."

PRAYER: Gracious Father, You know how difficult it is for me to see myself as I really am. Help me to be honest with myself — even ruthlessly honest. For I want to be as honest as You. Help me in this hour of challenge. For Jesus' sake. Amen.

FURTHER STUDY: Gen. Ch. 3; 2 Cor. 2:11, 10:1–6, 11:3 & 14
1 *What was Satan's approach to Eve?* 2 *How could Eve have overcome his strategy?*

DAY 21
Dealing positively with doubt
ACTS 17:1–15

"...they ... examined the Scriptures every day to see if what Paul said was true." (v. 11: NIV)

Today we face the question: what do we do when we find ourselves in the same position as the disciple Thomas — assailed by honest doubt? Well, first we must recognise that *doubts can be valuable if they motivate us to search deep and long for the answers.* Perhaps it was this thought that led Samuel Coleridge to say, "Never be afraid of doubt ... if you have the disposition to believe."

Unfortunately, there is very little sympathy given to those who doubt in most evangelical churches. Doubters are about as welcome in some congregations as a ham sandwich in a synagogue! It was because of the lack of concern shown in many churches toward those with honest doubts that two American

missionaries, Francis and Edith Schaeffer, set up their ministry in a remote Swiss village many years ago. They established a centre for those with doubts about their faith and called it *L'Abri*, which is French for 'The Shelter'. Hundreds have made their way there over the years, and have come back with their doubts resolved.

Have you ever heard of Frank Morrison? He was an agnostic who, many years ago, set out to demonstrate the validity of his doubts about the resurrection of Christ. The more he looked into the facts, however, the more convinced he became that Christ actually did rise from the dead. He finished up writing a book entitled 'Who Moved the Stone?' which is one of the greatest evidences for the resurrection I have ever read. There are clear answers to all the doubts you may have concerning the Christian faith. Search for these answers, and the more you struggle, the stronger will be your faith.

PRAYER: Father, help me today to understand that all things can contribute to my faith, including my doubts. When I realise this, then I will go far. Thank You, Father. Amen.

FURTHER STUDY: Matt. 14:22–36, 21:21–22; Lk. 12:29; Heb. 11:6; Jas. 1:6–8
1 *What did Jesus teach about doubt?* 2 *What causes doubt, and how should it be dealt with?*

| DAY 22 | **John's doubts about Jesus**
MATTHEW 11:1–11 |

"...'Are you the one who was to come, or should we expect someone else?'" (v. 3: NIV)

We continue meditating on the subject of doubt. An important thing to remember in relation to this issue is the fact that, although God would prefer us to believe, *He is exceedingly loving and gracious toward those who struggle with genuine and honest doubts.* Did you notice, when we were looking at Thomas the other day, that Jesus did not reject his doubting attitude, nor did He refuse his request for physical evidence that He was truly the Christ? Instead, Jesus said to him, "Put your finger here; see my hands. Reach out your hand and put it into my side. Stop doubting and believe" (John 20:27, NIV).

The passage before us today tells of another occasion when one of His followers became oppressed by doubt. John was in prison, and probably suffering great discomfort and disillusionment. John's messengers came to Jesus, wanting to know whether He really was the Messiah, or whether they should be looking for somebody else. John, you remember, had baptised Jesus and had introduced Him to the world with these words: "Look, the Lamb of God, who takes away the sin of the world" (John 1:29, NIV).

Does it not seem strange that John, who witnessed the descent of the Holy Spirit upon Jesus at His baptism, should now have doubts about who he was and the validity of His mission? How did Jesus respond to this situation? With tenderness and sensitivity. He said, "Go back and report to John what you hear and see: The blind receive sight, the lame walk, those who have leprosy are cured, the deaf hear…" (vv. 4–5). Our Lord could have rebuked the doubting disciple with strong words of reproof, but He didn't. Although He cares about problems, He cares more about people.

PRAYER: Thank You, Father, for reminding me that You see me, not as a problem but as a person. I know You are concerned about my doubts, but You are more concerned about *me*. I am deeply grateful. Amen.

FURTHER STUDY: Rom. 8:18–39; Jn. 8:1–11 & 3:16–17; Rev. 12:10
1 *Who condemns us?* 2 *How did Jesus respond to the woman caught in adultery?*

DAY 23

Decide to believe
JAMES 1:2–12

"…when he asks, he must believe and not doubt…" (v. 6: NIV)

Another important principle to employ when dealing with honest doubts is this: *make a conscious decision to doubt your doubts and believe your beliefs.* Living an effective Christian life, as we have been seeing, depends on how willing we are to exercise our wills in favour of God and His Word. To do this, of course, requires faith — faith in the fact that God has revealed Himself in His Son and through the Scriptures.

As a teenager, I had many doubts about the Scriptures but, one night, I made a conscious decision to accept them as the eternal and inerrant Word of God. Notice, I said 'a *conscious* decision'. In other words, I *decided* by an action of my will to doubt my doubts and believe my beliefs. I then found an astonishing thing. Both doubt and faith are like muscles — the more you flex them, the stronger they become. I had been using the muscles of doubt to a great degree, but unfortunately, I had failed to exercise the muscles of faith. When I made up my mind to accept the truth of God's Word by faith, muscles I never thought I had began to function.

Now, nearly forty years later, those muscles are developed to such a degree that I find, where God is concerned, it is easier to believe Him than to doubt Him. I trace the beginnings of my own spiritual development to that day long ago, when I decided to take what one theologian called 'the leap of faith'. Perhaps today might become a similar day of decision for you. I have asked you to make decisions about a lot of things. Make one more today. Decide to doubt your doubts and believe your beliefs. Now!

PRAYER: O God, perhaps this is the secret: I have used the muscles of doubt more than the muscles of faith. From today, things will be different. I decide to take You and Your Word on trust — now let it work. Amen.

FURTHER STUDY: Heb. Ch. 11; Matt. 15:21–28, 17:20; Rom. 10:17, 12:3
1 *What different aspects of faith are shown in Hebrews 11? 2 How did the Canaanite woman overcome the obstacles that confronted her?*

DAY 24
Do your emotions take over?
PSALM 103:1–22

"...the steadfast love of the Lord is from everlasting to everlasting upon those who fear him..." (v. 17: RSV)

We continue exploring ways in which we can turn deep and disturbing doubts into footstools for our faith to kneel upon. Another point we should keep in mind in relation to this question of doubt is that *some doubts are rooted more in the emotions than in the intellect.*

Our emotions are an important part of our being, and they can do much to make our lives either miserable or meaningful. When emotions take over, they cause our thinking to waver, so that we can come to faulty conclusions about life. Ask yourself this question now: am I a person who is ruled more by my emotions than by my intellect? If you are, then it is likely that your doubts are rooted more in your feelings than in your mind.

Many years ago, a Christian university student came to me complaining that he had serious doubts about the inspiration and reliability of Scripture. As I counselled him, I heard the Spirit say, "This is not an intellectual doubt, but an emotional one." I explored with him the area of his feelings, and he confessed to me that he could never remember a time in his life when he ever *felt* that he was loved. When the emotional problem was resolved, his doubts vanished of their own accord. His problem was not intellectual, but emotional. Reason and emotion are both important in life, but decision, especially decisions about the Christian life, must be built, not on what we *feel* to be true but what we *know* to be true.

PRAYER: My Father and my God, help me trace my problem to its roots and meet me at the point of my deepest need. This I ask in Jesus' Name. Amen.

FURTHER STUDY: Job Chs. 1–3
1 *What were some of the feelings Job expressed?* 2 *Did he allow them to give rise to doubt?*

DAY 25
Thomas, the doer
ACTS 1:6–14

"…you will receive power when the Holy Spirit comes on you; and you will be my witnesses … to the ends of the earth." (v. 8: NIV)

We spend one last day exploring the insights and principles which enable us to overcome doubt and develop our faith. The final principle we look at is this: *recognise that if you could not doubt, you could not believe*. So don't be threatened or intimidated by your doubts. Robert Browning put it like this: "You call for faith: I show you doubt, to prove that faith exists. The more of doubt, the stronger faith, I say, if faith o'ercomes doubt." Those who doubt most, and yet strive to overcome their doubts, turn out to be some of Christ's strongest disciples. We began this week by looking at Thomas the doubter, but we must end by looking at Thomas the doer.

One commentator points out that Thomas, being a twin, must

have developed an early independence of judgment that made it possible for him to break with his brother and become a follower of Jesus. This is an assumption, of course, but I think it is a valid one. It was that independence, perhaps, that led him to reject the testimony of the other disciples when they said, "We have seen the Lord."

Jesus did not reject Thomas because of his doubts, but said to him: "Reach out your hand and put it into my side. Stop doubting and believe" (John 20:27, NIV). Suddenly his doubts vanished, and he was transformed in that moment into one of Christ's most committed disciples. Up till then, no one had called Jesus 'God'. They had called Him, 'Messiah', 'Son of God', 'Son of the Living God' — but not 'God'. Here Thomas the doubter leapt beyond the others, and became the strongest believer of them all. And this faith of Thomas' did not stop at faith — it resulted in mighty achievement. The doubter became a doer. And how!

PRAYER: O God, what a prospect — my faith, at first so tentative, can, through Your illumination and my response, become a driving force. It can not only save me, but send me. May there be no limits! Amen.

FURTHER STUDY: Matt. 8:1–13; Rom. 10:17, 14:23; Heb. 11:1
1 *Where does faith come from?* 2 *What did Jesus say to the centurion?*

DAY 26

Why are Christians not exempt?
MATTHEW 5:38–48

"…He causes his sun to rise on the evil and the good, and sends rain on the righteous and the unrighteous." (v. 45: NIV)

We are meditating on turning life's difficulties into what Spurgeon described as "footstools for our faith to kneel upon", and we have discovered that although life deals blows to us all, those who meet life with the right responses and the right inner attitudes are those who turn their weaknesses into footstools.

I know some Christians who believe that they ought to be exempt from the cruel blows of life. I heard of a young man who was stunned after failing his examination and said, "I cannot understand. I prayed very hard before the examination, and I lived an exemplary life for the Lord. Why, oh why, should He fail me at this important moment?" Later he confessed to a friend, "As a result of God letting me down, my faith in Him has been shattered."

I can sympathise with the young man's feelings, of course, but I cannot agree with his conclusions. Suppose prayer alone could enable us to pass examinations — what would happen to the human race? Prior to examination time, classrooms would be deserted, and everyone would flock to the churches for prayer and meditation. Not a bad situation, you might think. But what would happen to the minds of young people if prayer *alone* brought success? They would become blunted by lack of study. I suspect the young man I have just referred to was depending more on prayer than on diligent and painstaking study. Now prayer *and* study make a good combination, but prayer without study never helped anyone pass an examination. Christians are not exempt from the natural laws that govern the universe. We may through prayer be able to overcome them, but we are not able to avoid them.

PRAYER: Father, thank You for reminding me that even though I am a Christian, I am still governed by natural laws that apply equally to everyone. I cannot be exempt, but through You I can overcome. I am so grateful. Amen.

FURTHER STUDY: Jas. 2:14–26; 1 Tim. 4:9–16; 2 Tim. 2:15
1 *What is James teaching us?* 2 *How does Paul apply this to Timothy?*

DAY 27

The end of the beginning
2 CORINTHIANS 2:12—3:11

"...thanks be to God, who always leads us in triumphal procession in Christ..." (2:14: NIV)

Today we come to the end of the theme on which we have been meditating over these past four weeks — "Footstools for Faith". Although this is the end of the theme, I pray that, for many of you, it will be the beginning — the beginning of a new approach to handling your weaknesses.

How thankful I am that, in the early years of my Christian life, God impressed into my spirit the truth that through my weaknesses, my strength could grow. I can almost pinpoint the day on which this truth was borne home to my heart. With just a few years of Christian experience behind me, I stumbled and fell. The temptation was to lie in the ditch and wallow in self-pity. But by God's grace, I got up, brushed myself down, and said, "Devil, you won that round, but I'll work on that problem until it is no longer a weakness, but a strength." I did work on it, and today I can testify that the weakness which caused me to stumble has indeed become a footstool. I say that humbly, recognising that the strength I have is not my own, but His.

Tomorrow you will begin a new day. How will you face it? Are you ready to face your weaknesses in the assurance that, no matter what life brings, you can turn every trial into a footstool for faith before God's throne? As your faith increases, so you can become stronger by your very weaknesses. Thus when you stumble, you stumble forward; when you fall, you fall on your knees and get up a stronger person. When we are Christians, everything is 'grist to our mill'.

PRAYER: O Father, I sense today that this is not the end, but the end of the beginning. From now on, I shall face the future knowing that every difficulty can become a footstool for faith. All honour and glory be to Your peerless and precious Name. Amen.

FURTHER STUDY: Eph. Ch. 3; 2 Cor. 12:9; Isa. 40:31, 41:10
1 *What was Paul's testimony?* 2 *What is your testimony?*